VISITATION

visitation   :   *a special dispensation of divine favor or wrath*
                       :   *a severe trial*
                       :   *an official visit for inspection or supervision*

VISITATION

Poems
JOHN GLOWNEY

Broadstone

Text & Cover Design by Larry W. Moore
Cover artwork adapted from
Petroglyph, Val Camonica, Italy;
CC BY-SA 4.0
Antropomorfi detti astronauti (b) - R 1 - Area di Zurla - Nadro
(ph Luca Giarelli)

Broadstone Books
An Imprint of
Broadstone Media LLC
418 Ann Street
Frankfort, KY 40601-1929
BroadstoneBooks.com

for

Professor Edmund (Ned) H. Creeth (1928–1997)

Do they hear us out there, like the little girl
at the bottom of the swimming pool
calling with the voice of water?

No one knows what succeeds.
It's technical.
The whale,
on that ancient ocean beach,

like a cripple
throwing away his crutches,

unhooks his legs.

*

> Any farm boy
> who has herded his father's cattle
> under the bountiful sun
> knows the hardness
> and shine of it

*

You begin sewing yourself
back together
with each nerve lighthouse
blinking its beam
through the fog of anesthesia, each breath
a kite
you can't see
jerking
at the other end of its long tether.

Ah. Ah. Ah. Ah. Ah. Ah. Ah.

Button-holes of pain
for wearing the shirt of another day alive.

Contents

THREE   *accidents of proximity*

ONE.

under a temporary sky

Break It, You Own It

Honestly, though, it was always broken,
which is the whole point, that is to say,
when this world first whirled
and popped into existence
out of nothing's sticky grasp,

the ur-broken thing, when it had wings
that glinted wildly in the suffused
and charged plasma, when it cascaded off
the cliff of itself
a mountain waterfall in native sunlight;
when the newly minted
honey bees, still smoking a little from
the tiny forges that made their immaculate
and fragile bodies, shook the pollen-dust
of a violet, left a tell-tale film
on the velvety atoms of air,

when the first honey bees
so insisted upon new life they went
flower to flower—back when this world wanted
to be called *Volcano of the Lilies*,
not *Rage Monster* or *Resentful Lover*, not *Plague Addict* or
Reservoir of Ashes—even then, broken, yet fresh
with new blooms,
it was yours.

SOME GIRLS

I can't read poems about crazy
girls, graphic, taut, well-written
poems about girls lit up, girls
on pills, crack, molly, crying
mascara, on the bathroom floor
of some rotted old hotel. Girls
who've pierced their nipples
with safety pins. Girls who piss
beside parked cars. Girls who
lie about their drinking, tell
the truth about their emptiness,
who lie about who they've fucked
and why they've fucked. Girls
who don't give a fuck. Fucked-up
girls. Whose mothers are sad.
Whose fathers wring their hands.
Who have tattooed their arm-pits,
shaved their heads, who
snarl when they kiss
someone. Anyone, really,
they'd kiss anyone who needs
a kiss, it's what
they have to give, and
they give it away
freely, all teeth
and bite.

When a Man Loves a Woman

Once, man and woman became one body,
a man *cleaved unto* his wife.

No one in Vegas drunkenly shouted
let's get married by Elvis.

Hotel rooms in Vegas did not pile up
to its pink neon panties dawn sky

with the bodies of strangers
newly christened
darling and *sugar* and *oh, baby.*

I've exclaimed *oak*
when I was seeking sweet shade from the elms,

whispered *moon* into the grass's ear
as we've lain together.

I've murmured *sister sister*
with my arms around any man,
his beard rough
against my cheek.

I've cried *good morning lover*
into the cave-mouth of the coffin.

And just last week,
when my wife said, *darling, sugar,*

could you run to the store for me?

I said, *oh, baby,*
of course.

KIN

Sun big as a fist in your face and tattered light
slurring out along the overgrown hedge
into the glare on the driveway. Washed-out

paint in narrow hallways, holiday meals
with uncles and first cousins
back from the war or prison,

the tattoo of family nailed to a shoulder
with a hard pack of smokes.
You've wandered back and forth

in these rooms for years, this house
where nothing else is,
the front door that opens, and opens

in, the rooms, these floors,
these rooms, the lying down together.
What doesn't matter most is here.

The sidewalk's unopened invitation.
And the '65 Fairlane that won't turn over,
no matter what is pulled out or put in.

Riding "it's a small world" at Disneyland, July 4, 2019

Mechanical puppets dressed in native costumes sing and dance.
Immigrant children in cages.
A "static" display of tanks arranged on the national mall.
Strap the buckle across your lap.
The Baby Trump balloon let loose.
The happiest place on earth.
Immigrant children swimming the Rio Grande.
Keep your hands and feet inside the ride at all times.
Southern California experiences a 6.4 earthquake.
Immigrant children strapped to their fathers.
Everyone's a foreigner in the Magic Kingdom.
Newton, Kepler, Herschel, Hubbell.
The earth remains motionless while its people move across it.
Immigrant children in cages.
Do not exit until your vehicle has come to a complete stop.
After the fireworks, the smoke remains.

Bleeding Out

Dear murdered people of the USA,
shut up.

Bang bang
was the big show,
was the gun whipped out,
was the speech made

to your itchy as a new shirt,
to your gravy drippings and birthday cake
and pain-killers and extra butter.

To your looking in the refrigerator at midnight.
To your wasting time at your desk.
To your *this pie is delicious* and your sleeping in.

Dear murdered people of the USA,
please do shut up now.

We are going to be right here all night
cleaning up this mess,

your dumpster fire of softly not breathing.

We're Pulling the Saints from the Rubble

We're blowing up theaters
in Paris, sending up ashes
from Bali, bombing churches
in Sri Lanka, blowing up Iraqi
weddings. We're turning our faces
away, listening for the sound
of an airplane against the air, in
a field, in the street, holding out
our hands to catch the falling,
we're pulling off concrete &
steel, we're giving the dead
the voice of concussion—which,
like music, is lost when released
into the air—we're collecting
their words, turning their faces
away, in a bazaar, next to us,
the tall buildings whispering
into the air, into our cell-phones
a conspiracy of collapse. Walls
and roofs make a loud dust,
un-frame in vectors of mortar,
cough up their nails; we're opening
the passengers' eyes for them,
lifting their arms, we're going
up and down the aisle
unbuckling their seat belts,
we are strapping another day
to their chests.

OUR REWARD

Our suffering is nothing special.
Look at the early saints, burned
in oil, riven limbs, intestines spilling
out like an uncoiled garden hose
from a bucket. Be grateful you're not
a jet-setter starlet, cheek-bones, blank
face, the paparazzi's ceaseless nattering.
Think of the laundromat in celebrity
heaven, dingy paint on the walls, noisy
driers that cheat you out of time, plastic
patio chairs, where the famous
wear shorts a decade out of fashion,
Rainbow Dash t-shirts, a bobby pin
stabbed into their unwashed hair.
Think of the wingèd cherubim, the Madonnas,
the Christ childs, eyes cast towards heaven
all these centuries, little gold halos,
knowing perfectly well what's coming.
Think of Saint Bartholomew strolling in
the door, flayed skin neatly folded
over one arm, smiling when he sees
the woman flipping through an old issue
of *People*, the row of empty machines.

SHELF LIFE

I was thinking about this clever monkey skill
we have for breaking open nuts and seeds

and animal bones and tossing the left-overs
out the cave window into a garbage heap

as big as any giant termite mound in Africa.
And how we thought we were so smart

with our inbred kings sitting in big drafty rooms
wearing ridiculous crowns

while we landed our ships on other people's shores
and ~~raped~~ claimed we owned them, and looted

in blood and small-pox. And how we sure knew
what we were doing pouring pavement

across every meadow, and feeding co2
to the Great Barrier Reef and the glaciers

of Antarctica until they choked. Trust me
when I say that jackals will not finish us off

by gulping down our marrow-bones, wind
and rain won't level our skyscrapers,

or booklice chew to pieces the words
of our impressive histories. Even when

we are gone, we'll still be here:
at the bottom of the Mariana Trench,

a plastic bag, flag of the race of humans.

COLTRANE EXHALES

I thought maybe he could blow it
all away, Trane and his sax,

wrenching the sickness up
through the horn's bell,

and not just the heroin
that lay like the corpse of a river

in his veins in those days,
not just that, but the sound

of the color black scraped
down to skin & nerve

& the booze to water
he blew straight,

the ache of the instrument
unloading its scales, the wetted

reed and embouchure and lips
pulling a snarl of notes

from the gut, that sweetness
at the bottom he practiced years to

and nowhere to go but out.

THE UNIVERSE

is a body shoved out of a plane
at 30,000 feet without a parachute,

sunk into the asphalt of a parking lot
like one of those sinkholes
in a Florida sub-division,

its broken bones pointing this way and that,
giving conflicting directions

about the planet's silky strand of orbit
wrapped around the sun,

                  but some lazy mornings
out on the lake fishing, admiring the sunlit dragonflies'
flint and strike,

the water-striders skidding along their thinnest of lines,

I remember how the universe pulled my body
out of nothingness,
and pounded and pounded on my chest
so I'd know it was love
knocking,

            and I took my first breath,
spitting up fish and seaweed—

and so now I kiss the universe full on the lips,

I give it mouth to mouth right back,

the only honest thing to do
when you owe a total stranger everything.

THE ALLIGATOR WRESTLER

It's not *really* wrestling.
The college boy's all jokey patter,

and 500 lb. "Charlie" just lies there
and takes it, thick-skinned, more straight-

man than killer, a long violin case mouth
stuffed with a piano keyboard of snaggle-teeth,

his first-generation brain circuitry
like that glitchy computer from the 80's

your uncle still uses. Our MC informs us
that a gator can go a year without eating,

can slow his pulse down to a single
beat a minute, will wait months

to strike his victim. But when the kid
sits on Charlie's back, hooks his chin

on the snout, and waves a hand around
inside that ancient jaw, our little crowd

flinches, then rewards him with applause,
a few bills in the tip jar. And afterwards,

we take the state highway, left over
from the 50's, out of the Everglades,

following the old trail to South Beach,
where we find a table and study

the crowded streets of tourists,
impatient, on edge, hungry

for the next astonishment.

On the Road, Montana

August a brush-stroke
of asphalt. Long slither

of rattler gashed into prairie,
the highway's a mirage we recite

to the clerk of miles. Mountains
dead-end in daylight, emptying

backwards and blind
into dry arroyos. Glass sky,

blown blue blur. We gas up,
candy bars, sour coffee,

drive 18 hours, find a cheap motel
in the folded ridge of foothills.

We sleep in a room
where we don't belong.

We close our mouths
over our solemn teeth.

Vanishing Point

A bottle of Coke and little donuts
from the gas station, vaping in the stalls
at high school. It's an open secret
our needs are endlessly unsatisfied,
like those sea-cliffs
pocked with nests of fledglings
and their traffic of birds.

Driving
while we searched the west coast
for the exact point of restlessness within ourselves,
we piled up radio miles of twangy girls
headed down the lonely trail
with the wrong cowboy,

then pitched our tent that first night
in sand
           to hear an invisible ocean
gathering and re-gathering.
                              Down the Oregon coast
with its guardian rocks,
ankle-deep in stale green waters. Sex
in a sleeping bag, hot and cramped, the night air
fog and wind.
                     We believed in
the highway, more restless
than we were, we let it pour us forward, white-striped,
patched, into the next day,

                              and the next,
long stretches interrupted by towns,
                 road crews raking steaming black pitch.
                 I read
my thin books of poems by flashlight,
fell asleep in awe of their moiled, sprung rhymes,

woke
before the Pacific's crescendos against my shore

before the tilted swells and troughs
arriving from beyond the last outpost of vision.

THAT SMOKY BEAT

That was off-center.
That was next in line.

That jumped too soon.
That was in-between.

That is the stubborn weed
of my heartbeat.

That let down its hair.
That I could only see through

the haze of trees.
That burns alone,

a cabin in snow.
That was unbalanced,

a tire rolling
over a curb,

its side-wobble.

Pale Blue Dot

It wasn't the worst place
except for the Neanderthals
wandering around
eating raw bear meat
and cave art
and then civilization
and ballerinas
who can't execute
a simple arabesque
and trip into the orchestra pit
and astronauts
who mentally checked out months ago
launched into outer space
after all these years in the jungle
ungrateful for beauty
killing each other
the same practiced motion
weightless men
at the tiny port-hole
looking back
at the earth's
slightly askew pirouette

A MAP OF AUSTRALIA

Hellish beauty—a map so crowded with fire
symbols they look like mushrooms
bunched along a tree root, or little geisha fans,

guitar picks, fish scales—red and yellow
clusters trimming a continent
with a ruffle of flame. A billion dead

animals littered over char, and abstracted
this way means I can't actually see
the carcasses but they say they are

saving a few: arboreal koalas, evicted
from eucalypt woodlands, wallabies,
of the Macropodidae family,

as are the singed kangaroos, marsupials,
the big jacks
with their long limbs bound and taped

like a prize fighter's hands.
I can't bear to look at them, anyway,
the cattle lying down in the smoke,

the glossy black cockatoo,
the Wollemi pines, conifers really,
secret canyon of stragglers, Lazarus

taxa, diaspora of the Cretaceous,
the ashy small towns, the panic-
stricken mothers on the beach,

hurrying to snatch up the smallest
children, rushing into the surf,
into rowboats. They are all

so out of place, the shelters
collecting handmade
joey pouches, all these wild things,

in the arms of medics,
or volunteers,
or the cold, frantic sea.

BURNING DOWN THE HOUSE

our house-

plants, their daily seances
in our rooms, their hours
and hours of meditative
poses. *They have feelings,*
my daughter tells me, young enough
to know. School-children
retrofit fish tanks into terrariums
for caterpillars, pill-bugs,
a grass-hopper. Old growth forests
change themselves into shadows.
The children bring more twigs and leaves.

*

The butcher works his messy
knife, frees the heart,
liver, lungs, kidneys, the chuck, the shank,
rib, round, flank.
What cannot be eaten?
Duck soup, caviar,
chicken feet, gizzards. Haggis, sheep's head.
Blood sausages, escargot, shark fin soup.
Rocky Mountain oysters. Calf brain, served
with tongue, sautéed with beurre noir
and capers—

*

The mansions of the Amazon are burning
Palm oil tears.

The mansions of the Amazon are burning
                              So much smoke
you can no longer see the jaguar, the gorilla,

the poison dart frog, hyacinth macaw,
golden-lion tamarind, the three-toed sloth.

The mansions of the Amazon are burning
The village roosters call out the names
of every dew-drop.

The mansions of the Amazon are burning

ALL OUR WORDS FOR MELTING

Once in the great big awful.
That's how it goes on the ice
floe so thin you can't. O dear
lover of pack ice, dear tusked
narwhal, O Steller's sea cow,
heavy-boned, fat and slow.
Great Auk, ext. June 1844,
we've reunited your skin
with your internal organs.
O Arctic Tern, O Arctic Fox,
God rest. Each and every
Eskimo Curlew, God rest.
Untended grave of any sea
creature, bless. Passenger
pigeon, *ectopistes migratorius*
in our living dead language,
we'll run a race in team t-shirts
hand-stitched by Mumbai
untouchables who work
for rusty tin cans, we'll
keep the Garden of Eden
in a jar of formaldehyde.
The scientific term for
attendance on this planet
is *weeping*. In the spring
migrations, the reindeer calves
drown in the thawing rivers.
May our story begin
"In the little village of words
called Inuktitut lives Tuvaijuittuq,
the place where the ice never
melts."

PROOF OF LIFE

Smutty prayers at the local bar by boys
who've lapsed into men, and night-time's

a tiny chapel where they drink to what
they don't feel, to unsolvable love,

the tab overloaded with middle age's
unsettled scores, the late hour's bitter

end: flop on the couch, flip on the tube,
the weekend's bummed-out fade out.

*

Modernity's apostles enter the past
without knocking, the inhabitants

as brain-washed as *1984*,
every recyclable syllable staked

to history's make-over, every old worry
out of warranty—

the customer service rep reads his script
from slave ship manifests,

three-fifth's men and women disembark in chains
at Charleston's docks, cotton's scars filigreed

inside their brains like a cattle brand.
We are the problem

for which there is no algorithm.

*

No need to apologize.
It's bad, people.
It's bad people.

Sackcloth and ashes for the sea-turtles.
Fleur du mal for the churches.
La mort for the tribes of snails.
Envy for the richest.

Debtor's prison for the coal miner.
Sun tan lotion for the beaches of Antarctica.
Polar bear steaks for all.

*

Honesty is what we demand.
A tally

of the oceans' droplets. Tail
the melted iceberg

to its final resting place. Play back
the security camera tape

of the rhino's horn and the poacher's
wild night.

*

A sliver of the oldest ice at the south pole
turns into a drop of water,

making a sound no one can bear to hear.
Civilization's demise bright

as the star of Bethlehem, the elephant
hears the fatal horizon arriving

in shudders of dust, the dung beetle
out of touch with the north star.

The earth is one long ransom note.
We've standing at the knife-

edge of birdsong, earthworm,
and honey-bee, the air littered

with the souls of extinct butterflies.

Peasant Scene

If Pieter Bruegel were painting me,
he'd scumble his canvas with the early
Monday morning meetings my boss loves,
and the starved dog my ex-wife pulled
from a dumpster in California that needs
arthritis shots once a week, and that
beautiful shirt I covet made by orphans
in Bangladesh working for $.03 a day.
He'd pose in chiaroscuro the woman
from accounting who likes to wear her skirt
like a short life lived without regrets
and the three A.M. call that my father's
not doing well; he'd cross-hatch me
taking the kids bowling, eating cereal
at midnight watching the black screen
of the microwave. For the goldfish
I spilled out, he'd feather in a swirling
cortege against white porcelain.
When it's finished, it will look a lot
like Bruegel's painting of the peasants
at a wedding, the way they go on
eating and dancing and laughing
even with the dark woods closing in.

THE CENTER HOLDS

I'm on my back porch taking pictures of myself
with a flash. The camera doesn't do me justice.
The angles are all wrong.
I can hear an airplane overhead churning through the tall fog
like a lawnmower.
Next door they've dragged a tv set out into the yard
and aimed it at the sky. *Lucy,*
Sergeant Bilko, the Ed Sullivan Show,
The Honeymooners untranslated, launched
into immortality. The oncologist says
he'll take another *look-see* at the x-rays.
It's probably nothing.
The flash pins me
against the photographic paper, like a beetle
from my 4th grade science project,
a few crystals afloat in silver salts.
There, do you see,
that dark blotchy spot?
The Milky Way's a circus tent overhead,
a field of wheat
before the scythe. Cathode rays
or vacuum tubes, the radio's static,
and that tv's still on the fritz. Once you're gone
who knows where you'll land,
Mars,
a study of cancer survivors, a Mexican clinic,
the extract of some Mayan root
in a glass of vinegar twice a day.
Each time you circle the sun, the runway
appears in a different place.
Place the wafer of light
that has journeyed unimaginable distances
on your tongue. Swallow hard
this forgiveness
you didn't see coming.

TWO.

patterns of astronauts

Moon

She is the daisy, all crude lines and crayon,
the first-grade boy drew for his mother.
She is a crumpled-up letter.
She is the reason why the teen-age boy throws the stone
at his father's eye.
She lights the red fox's fur crossing the meadow,
a silvery line ghosting bearded grasses.
She stalks lovers and murderers.
Her appearance and disappearance is a repeated chant,
ancient breath of some greater lung.
Stone-faced vamp, store-house
of whispered confessions.
Shrunk thin as a razor cut, or ballooned
big as a giant squid's eye,
she returns every night to the sky out of spite,
because she loves
what she cannot escape.

At Perihelion

Come at me, o shooting star
bearing the stony ore

of a shattered birth, come at me
raw & frozen & bitter-

tongued, follow the sound
of my blood in its moat, come

with tidal cry in my ear, bring
the rhythm of the guillotine, end

daylight's false comfort, the under-
tow of minutes, come at me

across the arena, bring a dust-
mote from the beginning

of time, lay darkness down
across space: come at me

in pieces, o fractured heaven,
drink this blue air

with your burning mouth.

Word of The Cure

The neurosurgeon water-witches the spot.
A small hole is bored into the skull

and the divining rod, a steel pin,
inserted. And, where elms and wheat fields

once swayed and brightened
in a glowing wave across the drive-in screen

of memory, the clinical stutter
of an electrochemical charge now flickers

onto a monitor. And just so, in another kind
of rapture, the jitterbug of impulses

through the hemispheres of the cerebrum
mindlessly falls into lockstep,

the wobbly hand finds hunger's bearings
and once again answers the mouth.

Word of the cure lets neighbors relax
their iron grip on their own hand-

to-mouth existence for a moment
and just talk, rumors over clotheslines,

the way, in Montana prairie country,
the first telephones let the local secrets

and sorrows pour through the survey-staked
barbed wire fences now doubling

as makeshift transmission lines.
And what was drilled into our thick souls

in Sunday School, the garbled sin of gossip,
what's left unsaid

of the day's hue and cry,
is strung along a boundary's fidelity,

the tattletale whisper
lingering in the long garlands of iron thorns and spiky stars:

the cloudy static of the human voice
stretched over the misery of distance.

Wings

Found like a busted sofa
put out on the curb for free. Pried open
like a radio,

the stations spilled out in a noisy mess. Message
in a bottle, the note
inside sloppily signed *ha ha*

by the elements. Still, we usually
don't bother with it,
little barn mouse, squeaky door

we keep meaning
to get to, neglected
until it springs a leak

and withers to a rag
snagged on a bush.
Then we fold the wings to the body,

bury it in a shoebox,
tell ourselves
it soars, there under the cold

rain, in the cold dirt,
there in the boundless
sky of earth.

the roller coaster at the amusement park
asks these days, but right now I'm flat
on my back, skivvies and socks, iodine
dye pumping through my arteries, all fifty
thousand miles of their many toll-roads,
the journey of living like this, whatever
this is, although it's certainly not anything
like the vacation trip that summer after
college, the stretches of desert highway
we sloughed off. Young, long-haired,
we took a few candids, nothing artsy or
the beauty-of-nature, but shots of us
at a gas station, a rest-stop, near dusty weeds
in a yellowed ditch, one of me on a back-
road I'd gotten us lost onto. We ended
with a walk along the Pacific, a beach
confettied with surfgrass, sea stars, kelp
and crab-shells, overseen by pelicans,
which is the way I feel lying here
in this huge CT scanning machine
as it forages my endless churning reach,
a tourist looking for shells, tallying
my algae blooms, riptides, muddy little
pools of hours. I'd found some sea glass
for a souvenir, but she'd said we could
never capture the day, how we felt,
we couldn't keep any of it. I tell the white-
coated technician that now he's seen
what I've got, and he says *who knows*,
maybe they missed a thrill or two,
and with that I'm out the door,
a bonus *keep on keeping on*
and thumbs-up, no sure thing,
the glow draining from my veins,
another day and what must
have moved Shelley's friend,

when the poet was cremated
on the beach at Viareggio,
to retrieve his unburned heart with a bare hand
from the fire.

*"Please scream inside your heart" is an appeal for silence on roller-coasters that comes
at the end of a four-minute video from Fuji-Q Highland (Japan) amusement park,
demonstrating COVID-era etiquette.*

THE BRIEF SUMMERS

He tells me he's watching a flutter of birds
he's never seen before, a little smaller
than a Steller's jay,
that have just dropped onto his deck
from a stand of spruce on the ridge
for the birdseed he put out yesterday,
right while we are on the phone.

He gets quiet for a moment,
studying a few dozen hues of brown wings,
tiny hollow bones for riding the updrafts,
spare little bodies. He's phoning down
to sea-level, where I am, from 11,500 feet,
the highest suburb of cul-de-sacs
in the world. There are higher single houses
.but this is the highest development. Big,
gorgeous three-stories, pavement,
power, cable.
                            From his deck,
he can see an uncluttered ten miles,
over the tops of clumps of towering evergreens,
down steep meadows, blue and red
with wild flowers that dissolve like sea-foam
in the brief summers,

the view telescoping into a valley now iced over
with the accumulations from the snowstorms
that blast through every few days. Yesterday
he snow-shoed out and skied all day
at Breckenridge. He never skied when
he was young, then took it up at 47, around
the time he remarried after his first wife
of 22 years divorced him. Vivacious new
woman, together they bought
this unbelievable place.

She has a non-small cell lung cancer
that started in her left lung, he explains.
Nothing she did brought this on.
More than fifteen per cent of lung cancers
occur in non-smokers.

His voice carries in the thin cold air
piled up for miles above the deck,
over the rasp of his skis in the powder,
breaking through the new snow
as he sails down the mountain,
feeling weightless in his bones.
The brown birds at his feet chirr
and peck at a marvel of seeds: millet,
flax, sunflower, buckwheat.

Epiphany in the Lobby of the Thornton Creek Multiplex Theater

When you are raised that John Wayne
is the keyhole through which all time
and space are framed, and now there are two
fellows in the movie theater lobby
who exchange a casual kiss,

that kiss is the bullet
that bears down on Wayne, grizzled, stoic,
only this time he stumbles,
and falls,

and the slender one, the other taller,
both of them,
and the girl behind the counter
in the pastel pink uniform,
and the stringy kid with the broom, and the woman

on her cell phone angry with her husband—
handfuls of clay and common earth,
mud and wattles, throbbing blood,
shaped to do only God knows what,

apparently to love,
only that, to love.

ILLEGAL

This is his passport to the door out the back,
the invisible kitchens of your motel, the yellow
cement block hallways, the ice machines, the mop
closets, the supply shelves crowded with cleaning
gear, detergent, the piles of wet towels
and dirty linens. And the next time you see him
he's crossing the parking lot with a power blower
on his back, pushing a whirl of newspaper fliers,
slurpie cups, and fast-food wrappers
like a shopping cart, an astronaut
ready to lift off over the tops of the long-haul rigs
and mid-size rental cars. The border runs up his arm
like a kiss of heroin, a sheared power line
flopping on the ground
along the road, lit up like a gas station
at night, official as a #2 lead pencil, a limp,
a bullet lodged in his skull.
Dumpsters line up like planets in his orbit.
And much later, when you're not there to spy
on him from your motel room window, strapped
into the cumbersome harness of his body,
floating at the end of his long tether,
he's got an oily rag out to polish the tall
flag-pole out by the highway,
he's rubbing down the gears and pulleys
behind the waving stars
and stripes, he's putting a small chocolate
wrapped in silver tinfoil
on your pillow.

TRANSLATION

She has no word for *office building*
where she spends her nights
cleaning, refugee

in the village of dimmed lights,
bagging the daily trash:
papers, pop

cans, fast food wrappers.
She is Hmong,
her lawyer explained,

sipping his bottled water,
a tiny woman lovingly erected
by the god of green terraces,

rice paddies, and the monsoon,
a wren of a woman
who bends over like grass

if passed along the road
by a fast Cadillac,
a little fish of a woman

who forded the Mekong,
a reed in its brown waters,
who listened in the camp

to the qeej musicians
ferrying souls along the spirit trails
to their ancestors, who sees

when she looks up not the sun,
but helicopters lifting off.
She landed at Sea-Tac

Airport, unclaimed baggage.
When the fields are exhausted
you move on, burn and slash,

plant again. Her teenage daughters
want tattoos. Her words are
bamboo thatch, monsoon rains

washing away fields
cleared with fire and long knives,
chicken entrails

fed to the village dogs, the blood
sweet and rich,
her words are melon rinds,

yams, eggplant tossed
to the chickens. The necklace she wears,
given at birth, warns away

bad spirits, says: I *am not a slave,
I belong to a family.*
With her three daughters,

she cleans *office buildings*
and she has no words for this:
the youngest girl, on a cell phone,

flirting in flawless English
with some American boy.

AMERICA COMES TO AMERICA

And what would you have done,
had you been there? Added some words
eliminating slavery, new paragraphs
about school shootings and queers
and term limits and abortion and abolition
of the electoral college...

*

—the illegals climb out
of the horse trailer, the way in
a night
wading through
miles of official darkness

*

the color of black shoe-
polish, of burnt almonds or
brown sugar, the color
of *colored*—this is the stuff

*

the energetic young park rangers
at Yellowstone can't find in
the informational pamphlets
in the pine-scented gift shop,

*

what washes ashore
when the levees fail
and let the waters in and in and in

*

what the local singer
at the minor league ball-game
is giving away for free

to the small crowd,
in that last high note,
just for showing up.

BUILD THE WALL

He's working a mini-cat
in cold drizzle, puffing a cig,
leaking smoke,
he's wearing long yellow waders
with suspenders
like he's ready for a day of trout fishing
in a Montana stream

only that's not on the schedule
today; today, it's a load of fresh dirt
to move around in the tiny front yard
behind the mostly-finished retaining wall

for the new construction
across from my place,
bigger than any of its neighbors,
buildable foot-print maxed-out,
                                        but not enough
grass lawn for a dog to piss on,

all columns and high ceilings, granite counter-
tops, all the up-scale
trappings made for pulling up the ladder and slamming
the door shut

on guys like Mr. Would-be Trout Fisherman here.

And I'm feeling morose and out of sorts,
trapped in my house now for nine months
and the holiday ahead looking pretty bleak,
and why did Jack, who lived there
in a little cottage until he was 94
but still sharp, sell anyway, and does this cold

and wet guy who's now beavering away
at getting the stones into that wall just right
realize he'll never be invited in, this is his last
visit,

although the short-fall in future visits
probably goes for me, too, and even though
it's not like the two of us,

Mr. Needs A Haircut and me,
will be getting together ourselves
anytime soon,

I have to admire what he's built,
Mr. Hacking Cough, Mr. Sopping Wet,
a big-shouldered wall, squared-up
to the sidewalk and to the grand house
going up behind it

that bespeaks respect for Euclidian
right angles and straight lines,
although he's not concerned
with their infinite reach,
no, his interest ends

where the property boundary
is marked with little red flags,
the exacting precision
of *trespass*,
of a never-ending line
between any two possible
points of connection.

Priced to Move

Which says stale bread,

which says homely child, which says
the foreclosure notice's burlap bag

of river rocks. And because
another person has failed

to buy my house, because there's nothing
I can't want on a summer afternoon

Simon says hold your breath
and touch the bottom

and *kick-the-can* and screened-in
porches and the sidewalk

getting lost like a baseball in tall grass.
And in a few weeks autumn

and kids with backpacks lining up
for school, and nobody having

squirt gun fights, or arguing over
ice cream—and because *there is nothing to do*

I close my eyes and count to 100
and keep them closed,

I *say when* the way twilight settles
on the parched lawns of the neighborhood

like the news of a coal mine disaster
in the faces of the waiting women,

say uncle
like the sound of a nail being driven true.

FREQUENCIES

A flock of notes has emigrated from Beethoven
to the Sex Pistols, and stands at the station
like freed Auschwitz survivors, blinking at the girl
asleep in a puddle of her own puke. Punk
chords thrown in your face like acid,
and the scarred disciples
gather in old hotel rooms
like lice or heroin addicts
where everybody sleeps it off
on one big mattress.
                        We fry pages of the dictionary
on a hot plate, nibble on the letter "Q"
for weeks, speak amongst ourselves a blood
tongue that sounds like wolves howling,
recite long sad poems to children
whose black clothes symbolize the end
of history. The days pass, forgotten
and beautiful.
                  Elsewhere.
                                 Satellites
crease the night sky
with patterns of astronauts.
                              There's always music
(wind-shiver, street shout,
        river whisper, murmur of planets)

and someone pounding on the wall
in the next room.
                        Itch of star-light.
We strap transistor radios
to our bike handles, ride out to the grass prairie
just beyond the porch-light,
sneak back home
with empty pockets
following the path of back porches.

No use crying.

　　　　　　　　　　Only tomorrow
will save this old world,
a sloppy Aretha torch song
playing over the loud-speaker
in the emptied-out stadium of the day.

Patterns of Astronauts

Through which hole would you insert
the soul?

*

*And they rolled the saint in black pitch
and set him on fire. He survived only
to achieve martyrdom by having his intestines
wound on a windlass.*

*

O Spotless.
O flutter.

Wasp in its paper nest,
pillar of salt.

*

Winched in, drilled in,
tunneled in, shoved

up the ass—one size fits all, the human vase.

*

Pressed for a comment,
the actress said
I am a prisoner of my lips and eyes and skin.

*

St John the Baptist found himself
in a hotel room in Tacoma
with a hooker in seven-inch heels. *Yikes*
he said. *Jumping Jehoshaphat.*

*

The skull is not designed to keep the brain in,
but to keep us from breaking in, tearing
the brain out by the roots, and stomping on it.

*

Self-trepanation lays bare the schematics.
Lays bare the mechanics of frame, joint; its flare &
flame, ballet of bone, tendon; confluence of old-
fashioned levers, its fire hose of impulses,
its electro-chemical cocktails—

*

You have to leave this lush planet sometime—
        the smallest hole in your suit
        and the enormous emptiness pours in
—like one of those tethered astronauts making repairs to his rocket ship,
        the blinking scribble of stars
        at his back—

bucketsful and bucketsful of it,
filling you up with eternity,
                        from which there are no known survivors.

THREE.

accidents of proximity

THE ENDS OF THE EARTH

Rod Stewart singing Maggie May.
Skinny boys in street-light,
old cars revved up, high
on beer, a little weed.
Night inched into night,
open all night.

*

Next town over, foreigners.
Greasers. Football game
fights. Watch out
in the locker-room.
We knew which ones.
If you went
to Detroit,
you'd be murdered.
Once we were born
here, we knew
what to think
about things.

*

She had a voice like mustard
and vinegar. Confession:
she scared me, driving
that station wagon in rain
dark as crow wings, bow-legged,
bad teeth. She took in
whoever showed up.

*

The war was in Vietnam.
The protesters were in Washington
or Chicago or New York or L.A.
We didn't know. Here
there was hay to bale,
tractors, milk cows,
corncribs, silos, granaries,
haymows. Here
only one boy
never came back.
The rest of us
buried
in this enduring soil.

*

I could drink water
pumped by hand
in the cup of my palms.
The taste in my mouth
was butter and milk;
it was wooly clouds that huffed east,
spattered thunder, lightning;
straw-dust, corn
pollen, hay chaff. I choked on it.
It fed me.

Giving Blood

Volunteers all: the white-haired nurses,
tan students, secretaries, wan businessmen
line up for blood-letting. No blood-factories,
but a cottage industry, piece-work laborers
paid in the coin of good citizenship. Have you
had sex for money or drugs in the last
six months, they ask, when the question
we should be asked is have we loved
for sex, did we embrace fully in
our hearts those whose bodies, in
carnal tide of night, opened
and flowed with our bodies, those who, much later,
having left our lives, leaving in us
this tattered hole that only rents and
unbinds further in the embrace of another,
pass without speaking, years later, in the grocery—
our blood still leaps, the passion-blush
rising in our faces.

The needle pricks, a cruel steel nail.
I am left to siphon off the leakage
of the heart-pump's suck and throw.

Drink ye all of this...in remembrance of me
but here among the disembodied rabble, the thieves,
the forgiven one and the unforgiven
one, indistinguishable, it is a scientific
transaction. No transubstantiation,
no priests to assist,

only nurses ministering sterile ligature.
Only the rooms of the heartbroken lying on cots.
Only the thin purplish-red line of blood force-fed

vein to vein and we are transported into
another's arms, this systolic embrace

of strangers binding us blindly
to another, this unrehearsed union
between the pulse of bodies,
another heart healing across the common darkness
with mine,

red, cadenced, blessedly anonymous.

MELVILLE IN PARADISE

The soul, neither animal, vegetable, mineral, is shunned in the material world.

Diaphanous orphan,
or the child left out of the game of kick-the-can,
crying under the porch.

A grand pronouncement spread like a cloud over the animal realm,
so useless, yet so undeniable.

And Melville, jumping ship
in paradise, transmuted,
the women, naked,
openly sexual,

or Beethoven hesitating over this note, the next
—base anguish given
angelic voice of disturbed air—
he marks it, erases it,
pens it in again....

What cannot be undone inside us becomes a choice.

The human approximation
of otherworldliness
            blinks open,
the physical aggregates around us,
ill-dressed in the scourge of whorish flesh.

Like sailors press-ganged with doctored drinks
            we are forcibly carried aboard, we awaken
            to years at sea, sick, misused,

we take up the whaler's ways,
we ride the hard ocean, tattoo ourselves
with secret symbols.

Until mid-life. Until now. We return,
the village uninhabited, the fields overgrown,
our wives with other men.

To whom can we explain these fresh appetites,
            what extremities
            we have seen with our own eyes,
 now that we have again stepped out
of the overturning surf
onto the beach and its hot white sand

an evolving music fluting
in the air within ourselves
                    that our mouths cannot yet sing.

STINGS

You fall when your life is over.
              Bahadur, Raji honey-collector

It is the path of the bees, nomadic,
the flowering of the great green forest,
that draws them, that charts a life, a way,
the secret of living by

what stings you, the smoke
in your eyes that lets you see
how the queen commands
the grand cottonwood,
the limb where she has gathered
all sweetness for her children,
each with an ordained berth
in this barracks of confection,
and the sticky prick of thirst
for the inflamed throats of flowers.

*

The stunned bees erupt, released in smoke and fire.
The honey-collectors plunder the high nests,
wring out the golden fruit into pots to sell.
The bees needle and stab, and the honey-collectors
retreat in the evening, fingertips smeared with honey,
their wrists jeweled with tiny stingers.
Sleep is a cloud of wings
humming and flickering in the mind's canopy,
an indulgence of the exquisite pharmacology of hunger
extracted from their meal of milky white wax
laced with red pepper and salt.

They do not become bees
but fall more and more in love
with the climb into the towering silk-cotton trees,

where the gods live,
a journey of many small wounds
they must take each day.

The Raji are a semi-nomadic ethnic group in Nepal who live primarily by following the bees as they migrate through the lowlands with the blossoming of flowers.
(National Geographic, June 1998)

TRUTH

I've accumulated months and years of it,

stuffed it into little drawers
and cannisters, tins and jewelry boxes,

crammed decades of it into trunks
and cartons and crates. And I was sitting

at the kitchen table making a list
when the Past strolled in the back door

and started in bitching about some insult
or slight from some party or barbeque

in 1973 nobody can even remember.
And the kids keep running in and out,

blinding light sprayed everywhere like water
from a sprinkler, and a house wren

on the lawn, asking nothing, and the tall spruce
beside the hedge, asking nothing,

the kids getting a drink of water
at the sink, laughing, making some crazy plan

for the afternoon, something to do
with string and popsicle sticks they've just

invented, letting the screen door slam,
tracking in dirt, running through

all that empty space, all that light.

KNOW THYSELF

is the vibe of the gang of philosophers
who crowd onto my bus this morning

with their skate-boards and flamboyant hair,
their wise-cracks and snickers and phenomenal

youthfulness. They give me the side-eye,
old guy, nice suit, briefcase, tie

knotted at my throat, sizing me up:
the years' grind, the acid drops,

heel flips, and ollies I didn't land.
They know there's not much

in this world worth the effort
except that moment of catching air—

it's like crawling under your own skin,
the way some Alaska natives, in winter's

deepest snow, will dig down
through blue ice to a rocky shore,

exposed when the salt-water ebbs,
to gather fresh mussels,

and staying there just long enough,
before the tide covers you,

on your little scrap of earth,
under a temporary sky.

The Math

The math tells us
we have to replace ourselves at such-and-such
a rate, to account for all the methods of dying.

We have our preferences, the way one might prefer Aunt Lillian's
rhubarb pie over Aunt Grace's apple, or peppermint-
flavored toothpaste to bubblegum. Natural death
by extreme old age is a big favorite, while head-on collisions with drunks
ranks at the bottom
                    along with childhood
leukemia, which took
my cousin at age 17, even after he had seemed,

that summer before--a tough spring—

to have been making progress with the chemo, too skinny
but his color was better,
all the aunties said hopefully
at the family reunion at the park,
                              with its big dumb watermelon smiles,
                              its three-bean salad days,
                              the new baby cousins.

        It's a day like this, once a year
all the distant relatives together, that makes the math
take a little break from carpentering
the old into the new,
pull a bright-red Farmer Brown kerchief from a pocket
and rub his eyes,
blubbery as a young boy,
noisily blowing his nose.
                        But the math is the math,
and it put a shoulder into it for Bryan
like it would for anyone,

plucking the bent nails
out of the splintery wood
of the used-up soul,
straightening them out, hammering them
in again,

the babies
being passed from lap to lap

       flawless as the noon sun on picnic tables
       pure as cold water from a hand-pump well

but with the tragedies of the past, fresh again, pounded into them.

Plume

When the worst kind
of brain tumor
gave our neighbor Noelle

a stroke,
the doctors sawed in, knifed
the skull, cut out

what they could. But this cancer
is stubborn and elusive,
like a bad memory, a cloud

plumed so deep
into the ventricles they couldn't
clean it all up

even if they had those over-sized janitor mops
and big mop buckets
with wringers

they use on high school hallways.
I can't bear to dwell
on the mechanics of cells,

how the bad ones
resist all orders, spread
through the body

like an ink stain,
how the brain
can't be welded

and straightened out
like my boyhood
bike's bent frame.

They've given her a shiny
new wheelchair.
And bald now for months,

all the chemo,
can she remember her hair,
how it felt

to wash it,
and to stand before the mirror
in a cloud of steam

slowly rubbing it dry
with a towel.

Forsaken

Tall stalks of young men tilt like silos.
The steeples of roots put down deeper
than drought. The fallow fields ring bitter,
vague with bird calls, lush rust of disuse,
the churches starved on *amens*, fat with guilt,
and empty. The auto factories walked off
in Flint and Ypsilanti and Detroit
like the last movie-goer exiting the theater,
the marquee burning last year's titles
—*Cadillac Fleetwood, Ford Thunderbird,*
     the El Camino—
The streets stayed behind, the sledge-
hammered neighborhoods anchored
like a needle in your arm. Sharp-
toothed dreams snap at themselves
on the cracked basketball courts
where boys soar into newspaper
headlines, dead or famous or both.
The two-lane stops at the county line,
the boarded-up union halls talk
in their sleep, the barn peak's rooster
fidgets like a little boy in a suit
at a funeral. It's shoeless midnight,
and the abandoned farmhouses
hold a last little warmth, tinder
of cravings, a smoky light:
the furnace of the human body
cooked to a rotten
shine, tooth, mouth, bone.

Mappa Mundi (excerpts)

A *mappa mundi* is a Medieval European map of the world, not
intended to be used as a navigational chart or to show relative
areas of land and water, but to illustrate different principles.

Here.

                                        Hard-scrabble

blistered summers, circadian,
oracular,
haze of the burled optic
nerve,

                        blurred ken of fissured synapses;

fed fundamentals of water and sun,
as if soil
was worked in, cuneiform on hewn stone,

seeded within me
this land

            rainstorms passing over the fields of the mind

no thought vast enough to explain

*

To trace a coast-line,
outlined by this or that incident, dull knife

slashing a riff-raff, sharecropper poetry
into the few acres
I knew,

granary, silo, the sheds of cattle,
ephemera of seed-husk, chaff,
time's chuff,

the dirt I was made of,
my résumé's muddy furrow,
        a farm to escape from.

*

              Came out of

a hundred acres
in the middle of Michigan

the map of which
smelled sweetly
of hayfields.

*

Crow-feather land,

a meditation
wide as the blue
shirt of sky above,

delta of raccoon teeth,
deer hoof,
rabbit bones,
bear scat.

Some afternoons
silence raged
for miles.

....

*

And how could we bear
not to fool with it—whatever
animal this was
shaped
into a small death—the hide
stiffened,
lying in the tractor wheel rut
for weeks,
guts spilled
and dried already, the leathery
whip of a tail

that felt strangely satisfying
in my hand
when I picked
it up and hurled it
—at the sky, at a brother—

Postcard from Paris

The other divorced man on my street is selling all
he can bear to part with.

Torn pieces of paper, scrawled with red crayon
and pinned or scotch taped on, value each item.

2 ties for a $1.

$15 OBO for a four-slice toaster.

Matching lions head bookends for $40.

Any magazine 25 cents.

I pick up a stack of unused yellowing postcards.

Greetings from Honolulu.

Beautiful San Francisco.

A smiling man and woman hold hands in front of the Eiffel Tower.

Wish You Were Here

A card table piled high with out of fashion
shirts and suits, cardboard boxes
overflowing like flowerpots with small gadgets,

more useless household goods
strewn across the tiny lawn
like rice after a wedding.

Driving Home

In the category of nobody knows how
these things happen, I find myself
on the road back from a friend's funeral
with a frog hanging from my pick-up's
double side-mirror, one long frog-leg
dangling above the ditch's drought-brown
grass. A tail of highway recedes into
the reflection's inner distance; there's also
a mail-box, a slice of side window
holding leaves, clouds, and in the top
mirror—pines, orange sunset,
telephone pole. He was barely hanging on
when they tried to fly him
to a Seattle hospital, the helicopter's
thumpthumpthumpthumpthumpthump
a heartbeat that roared across the sky.
Lives blur off into the obituary's
skid-marks. Everybody cries, then genuflects
at the wayside shrine of *glad it wasn't me.*
It's late summer here, the evening
spills *darkness*, the soft dusk enters
the leaves, the earth's embankments.
That frog's grip on the *now* will
soon slip: the motorcycle cop
drinking coffee in a donut shop,
nose in the race-track betting guide,
leaps to his feet when I cruise by,
on the phone with one hand,
a drink in the hand I'm holding
out the window, steering with my knees.

LOTTERY TICKET

It is in these moments—we may be eating toast
or watching a bicyclist

navigate evening traffic in the setting sun—
when the possibility that our lives

could still turn out differently
is so powerful and real

that the impulse carries us away,
as it does the elderly couple

on the bench outside the seven-eleven,
leaning over the lottery ticket

they have just purchased,
scraping away the silvery veneer

that hides millions, or nothing,
probably nothing, lost in the moment,

the man's thinned, combed-over hair,
the small bag of groceries at their feet,

like schoolchildren, diligent and absorbed,
intent at their coloring books,

when the sky can be a thick waxy pink,
the grass scribbled purple,

the grazing cows shaded a calico mix
of red and yellow, and the sun,

stubbornly violet, bursts in rough strokes
through its perfect circle,

its pointed rays,
green the chosen color,

stabs the hillsides
and a distant forest, smudged magenta.

ADVICE

Of course they wished me wealth and stuffed
a wad of forged bills and wooden nickels

into my pocket, and they wished me much
success in adding up the tally of hours

hung out like a clothesline of wet laundry
between the screw and the rack and yes

they said you can arm yourself
with only a tea spoon and drown

in any salty sea you can fill
with your own tears and sorrow

is a goat path deep into the mountains
you follow with your eyes shut tight.

And yes they assured me bad luck
roosts with its back to the north wind

and when your head refuses the sandals
your bare feet offer you may one night

find yourself standing under stars
thick as a cotton field

in the charcoal ruins of the sky,
impenetrable, beautiful, unimaginable,

trembling like a compass needle
feeling its way into the dark,

the way it is when your heart
is engorged on love,

about which nobody said a word.

VISITATION

My neighbor tonight is in his underwear
carrying out a bag of trash, a working-class
Santa, no robe, his spindly calves
catching the sequined moonlight
like the face of the sickly kid
in the war movie on the late night
you know will freeze up in the big battle.
He is not drinking or cursing the dark
or taking a drag on the faint fire-fly
of a cigarette; he is just crossing
the cracked and scored rectangle
of the driveway/basketball court
wearing only white underwear
and a pair of flip-flops that make
an odd little tune, clip-clip, scrape,
clip-clip, above the canned applause
of a tv show looping out of the window
into the zombie slave glow of tonight's
stars. And to the other hierarchical
order of almost but not quite invisible
beings for whom he's carrying this load
of manna, to this unwashed audience
awaiting bread crusts, coffee filters,
banana peels, grapefruit rinds, left-over
chicken pot pie, his mind is
great and unknowable and terrible
and his thoughts play the die
of chance or fate, and what he
empties into the metal can may
not be enough, or may not be in
time, or will not last until the next
visitation, but he has risen anyway
from his tv and his bag of potato chips
as if he understood the role of a god
is to atone for his long absences.

Acknowledgments

The following poems in this collection (several in earlier versions) have previously appeared in the journals listed below, and their publication is gratefully acknowledged here.

32 Poems ("Wings")
The American Journal of Poetry ("Translation")
The Baltimore Review ("Truth")
The Birmingham Review ("Stings")
The Bitter Oleander ("Shelf Life")
Cloudburst ("At Perihelion") (forthcoming)
Juxtrapose ("Lottery Ticket")
Mid-American Review ("Word of the Cure")
New Ohio Review ("Break It, You Own It")
Passager ("Driving Home"; "Epiphany in the Lobby of the Thorton Creek Multiplex Theater")
Poetry Northwest ("Illegal"; "Melville in Paradise"; "Giving Blood")
Pontoon ("Visitation")
Shenandoah ("Moon")
Tar River Poetry ("The Center Holds")
ZYZZYYVA ("Advice")

ABOUT THE AUTHOR

John Glowney's work has appeared in *North American Review*, *The American Journal of Poetry*, *Shenandoah*, *32 Poems*, *Michigan Quarterly Review*, *River Styx*, *Mid-American Review*, and many other journals. He is a recipient of a Pushcart Prize, Poetry Northwest's Richard Hugo Prize, and the Poetry Society of America's Robert H. Winner Memorial Award. He lives in Seattle.